I0434376

Tenets for the Tea Party
Proposed Solutions and Priorities for a Complicated World

By Othello Mandelaous Pi

This book sets forth 20 proposed solutions to current problems faced by Americans, with these 20 proposed solutions divided into 8 parts. These 20 solutions are suggested thinking points, starting places, and hopefully the community discussion that ensues around each solution will generate new ideas and answers expressed in a constructive manner.

This book does not purport to speak for the Tea Party (or for any party) – rather it is the intention of this book to be of service to the Tea Party and to all Americans, to help crystallize our thoughts and express our goals in the vocabulary of a complex world.

ISBN-10: 1467999075
ISBN-13: 978-1467999076

DEDICATION

To those of us wishing to thrive, contribute and work diligently in a fair environment that supports our success.

THESE TENETS FOR THE TEA PARTY ARE THE FOLLOWING 20 POINTS:

INTRODUCTION

The United States is a country founded on great principles and a unique balance of diverse powers. Our Constitution does an admirable job balancing a myriad of interests and needs – in the United States Constitution you will find a balance of government and the individual, of Congress, the White House and the Supreme Court, and of State government and Federal Government. We enjoy freedom of speech, which makes this book possible.

Now we find ourselves in difficult times, but also times of great opportunity to make important, useful change, and a time of introspection. In recent years, Americans have witnessed a severe financial crisis, a terrible oil spill in the Gulf, huge Ponzi frauds, high foreclosure rates, and devastating unemployment. Many of these problems arose because both individuals and entities have gamed the system, putting self above ethics, others, community. No system, even one as great as that of the United States, can function properly if organizations and people game the system.

It is relatively easy to express the big-picture problems we Americans face. It can be hard, especially for ordinary citizens without in-depth experience or access to inside government and corporate information, to propose comprehensive solutions. In these pages you will find detailed descriptions of specific problems in the U.S. financial, tax and political systems, with specific proposed solutions.

This book does not purport to speak for the Tea Party, but the hope of this book is to be of service to the Tea Party, and to all Americans, to help crystallize our thoughts and express our goals in the vocabulary of the complex financial world.

GOALS WORTHY OF EXPRESSION

The United States government needs to WISELY trim spending if possible, and we need to raise tax revenues. The United States government also needs to foster growth, innovation, and jobs, without sacrificing long-term objectives such as financial stability or our environment.

This book stands for the proposition that what America needs are BOTH enhanced government effectiveness AND refined budgetary surgery cutting the spending we have. What America does not need are easy-to-say-but-drastic-to-implement solutions that involve wholesale cutting of government departments or sacrificing programs for the needy or ruining the environment. What America does NOT need is wholesale tossing of a brilliant government structure that would work well if fewer people gamed the system. Yes, it *IS* harder to come up with refined surgery to balance our budget, but just because it is hard does not mean it is not worth doing. We CAN do this – we need our leaders to step up to the plate, put partisanship aside, and work together using the best minds at their disposal as consultants.

As our politicians grapple with how to balance the budget and raise more tax revenues (Obama's tax the rich vs Bachman's tax the impoverished at least a little bit), this book offers a proposal that blends some tax proposals with refined budgetary surgery, in hopes of creating a better, more sustainable economy, existence and environment for all Americans. This book doesn't have many pretty slogans, but it does offer solutions that are worth exploring.

For those of you that fear that anything put forth by any one of the Tea Party is all about wholesale cutting of social programs, please know that this book is not advocating saving tax revenues at the expense of social programs; this book is advocating a more precise, thoughtful approach to taxation to pay for whatever EFFECTIVE spending priorities there come to be. A terse review of spending and a more thoughtful taxation approach are not mutually exclusive ideas.

What follows next are the 20 points of the proposed Tenets for the Tea Party, divided into 8 parts. These 20 points are suggested thinking points, starting places, and hopefully the discussion that ensues around each point will generate new ideas and solutions.

PART 1 – FINANCIAL REFORM

Our government and our culture need to reward and support integrity in business (the ends do not justify the means), thus stabilizing and rebuilding confidence in the financial markets. This is also a role of the President and other leaders, to highlight and thus encourage ethical business behavior that supports community as well as shareholder wealth.

Beyond this, it is clear we need prompt, specific and serious reforms of the financial system. Many of us can express this in big picture words, but don't have the hands-on experience to say in simple terms what this means. This book proposes the following:

1. **Eliminate Insider Trading by Congressmen**

   Insider trading is illegal under the securities laws – except for Congressmen! Right now, our Congressman can legally do insider trading. In other words, a Congressman legally can know that a bill/legislation/funding/government contract will be voted on, and that Congressman can also know how that vote will impact certain publicly traded companies, and then that Congressman can legally invest (or sell) those publicly traded companies, even though that Congressman has inside information (due to his role as Congressman) that the rest of us don't have. Studies have shown that investments by Congressmen regularly do better than if someone had invested in a stock market index generally, which is statistically impossible without inside information. This ability of Congressmen being able to trade on inside information is often cited as one of the reasons that a Congressman who began with relatively humble means can leave Congress extremely wealthy. It is a bad thing because it gives Congressmen a legal financial incentive to vote for what is best for their pocket book/stock holdings instead of what is best for their constituents.

SOLUTION: Congress needs to pass a law making insider trading as illegal for Congressmen as it would be for any corporate insider. If there is any insider trading by a Congressman, part of the remedy needs to be that the profits from insider trading are disgorged to the taxpayer – i.e., these insider trading profits would be paid to our government to reduce the deficit, etc.

2. **Eliminate High Frequency Trading Manipulation**

Investors ideally invest – i.e., put money into companies in exchange for stock – in order to give companies money to grow with. In exchange, investors seek a return on their investment – such as dividends or increases in the stock price. Investors investments help companies grow, but understandably investors are reluctant to put money into a stock market that is not stable or that is easy to be gamed/manipulated by others. On May 6, 2010, the "Flash Crash" occurred and shook the financial markets to its core. In the course of minutes the stock market (the "Dow Jones Industrial Average") dropped by a HUGE 9% (a drop of more than 1000 points), and then bizarrely recovered much of that drop in minutes. This huge vacillation cost some well-intentioned honest investors huge losses while other investors made huge profits. Regulators found that high frequency traders were a part of the Flash Crash problem. High frequency traders are people that have special access computers to the investing system that ordinary investors don't have, which gives them an unfair trading advantage to the ordinary investor. High frequency traders use this special access to invest in companies for mere seconds to take advantage of tiny movements in stock prices by doing huge volume trades, as opposed to traditional investors who invest to give a company operating capital. High frequency trading actually accounts for over 70% of equity trades taking place in the US, so therefore has a huge impact on the stability of the stock market. High frequency traders seek just a fraction of a penny per share on every trade, and high-frequency traders move in and out of their trades so quickly that they can execute thousands of trades on the same stock in just one day! Many say that high frequency traders sometimes "stuff" the investment pipeline by submitting orders in batches that the high frequency trader doesn't ever intend on executing. More specifically, the high frequency traders sometimes send stock buy (or sell) orders at prices that makes these orders non-executable - meaning these "stuffed" orders are orders to buy or sell stock that have execution prices outside the bid-offer spread. The high frequency trader then quickly cancels these orders to avoid risk of actually executing on them. The stuffed orders can clog exchanges and create pricing noise that prevents clarity in the markets.

SOLUTIONS:

● Outlaw stuffing orders and require firms to report the number of orders having execution prices outside the bid-offer spread that were submitted but then promptly cancelled

● Require all stocks be held for no less than 10 minutes

• Make special access to the financial markets a highly regulated privilege that can be revoked when it is used to manipulate or game the market

3. **Regulate Credit Default Swaps.** Credit Default Swaps (sometimes called CDS) were a major factor in our financial crisis and could easily still cause another financial crisis. As explained in more detail below, credit default swaps are used by many investors to place a bet that a certain borrower will default on their debt. By the end of 2007, the outstanding amount of credit default swaps (essentially bets) was an astounding $62 trillion. Even now, after the financial crisis, there are still a staggering $26+ trillion of credit default swaps! Keep in mind that the whole US economy (measured by gross domestic product (GDP)) in 2010 was only $14.7 trillion. In other words, just by looking at the numbers, there is no way still for the companies issuing these credit default swaps to actually pay all these bets off should the need arise. In other words, the credit default swap issue is still here, unaddressed!

As more detailed background, a credit default swap is like an insurance policy that says that if a borrower defaults on his loan, the insurance company will pay the loan to the holder of the credit default swap. For this promise, the insurance company gets an insurance premium from the holder of the credit default swap. However, there is a HUGE difference between a traditional insurance policy and a credit default swap – ANYONE can purchase a credit default swap, even if they are not the lender on the loan to the borrower! In fact, there can be multiple credit default swaps sold to many different credit default swap buyers, none of whom are directly involved in the loan at all! These credit default swap buyers are willing to make a bet on whether the borrower will default, and the price of the bet to the credit default swap buyer is the insurance premium they need to pay to get the credit default swap.   In other words, a credit default swap is like saying you could buy insurance on my house even if you have no interest in my house. If my house burns down, you get paid! In fact, a hundred people could each buy that type of insurance on my one house, even though not one of the insurance buyers has any interest in my house, as long as each insurance buyer is willing to pay the insurance premium to the insurance company. In the credit default swap context, that means one insurance company can offer loan default insurance to 20 different people that a borrower won't default on the borrower's debt. If the borrower doesn't default, then the insurance company (such as AIG) gets to keep the premiums from all those credit default swap buyers willing to make the bet that the borrower would default. If the borrower does default, then suddenly the insurance company is on the hook to pay all those people who bought credit default swaps MILLIONS of dollars, far more than the insurance company might even have reserves to pay. That is why AIG was in such bad shape – if they had only offered credit default swaps to the actual lender on the loan, rather than also to credit default swap buyers willing to make a bet, then likely AIG would have been fine and not needed a tax payer bailout, but instead credit default swaps were offered to many many credit default swap buyers beyond the actual lender.

Shockingly, not only can large numbers of individual buyers purchase a credit default swap based on a single loan, even if not one of those credit default swap buyers is the actual lender of the loan, but also, and even more importantly, <u>there is no required reporting of credit default swap transactions to any government agency</u>! Not even the SEC! Credit default swaps are also not traded on a securities exchange, so credit default swaps are not even subject to reporting requirements that securities trading exchanges require.

Also noteworthy, credit default swaps are also used to structure synthetic collateralized debt obligations (sometimes called CDOs). An example of a synthetic collateralized debt obligation is Abacus 2007-AC1, which is the subject of the civil suit for fraud brought by the SEC against Goldman Sachs in April 2010. Abacus is a synthetic credit default obligation made of credit default swaps that referenced a variety of mortgage backed securities.

The vast dollar amount, in the trillions, of credit default swaps, when combined with the complete lack of reporting requirements on credit default swaps and the incredibly long tentacles of credit default swaps throughout our economy (even used in other derivative securities such as collateralized debt obligations), makes this a high priority item that needs to be addressed. For example, one of the reasons no one is able to say for sure what the impact of a Greek or Italian or Spanish debt default will be, is no one knows for sure how many credit default swaps have been written on that debt, or by who. Any institution that wrote credit default swaps on that European debt might fail if those countries default on their debt, taking all their other businesses down with them, hurting shareholders, 401ks, etc., just as with our recent financial crisis. The lack of clarity in how many credit default swaps there are on any issue (such as the current concerns over the impact of Greek or Italian or Spain debt defaults), the lack of reporting to the SEC and the associated lack regulation by the SEC of credit default swaps, and the huge trillions of credit default swaps still in use today, make credit default swaps a real problem for our financial system and United States stability.   That is why Warren Buffet called them and similar derivatives "weapons of mass financial destruction" all the way back in 2003. It is clear that the lack of transparency of credit default swaps, when magnified by the multi-trillion dollar size of the credit default swap market, poses a systemic risk to the United States economy.

SOLUTIONS:

- No entity should be allowed to issue credit default swaps if that entity will be unable to pay the obligation they create, and any entity issuing credit default swaps should be required to maintain reserves to pay off the credit default swaps.
- Credit default swaps should be regulated as a security, subject to the Security

and Exchange Act of 1933 and the Securities Exchange Act of 1934. The SEC should be the overseeing regulatory authority.

- The purchase of credit default swaps should be limited to those having an actual interest in the underlying security/asset — such as only the lender of the loan can purchase a credit default swap in the event that the borrower on the loan defaults.

4. **Tax Corporate Coffers Housed Offshore.** United States corporations can legally earn revenues overseas, and if the US company parks that earned revenue in an offshore entity, then that US company will not pay any US taxes on that revenue. For example, a US company can create an invention here in the US, get a US patent on the invention, assign the US patent to an offshore entity that the US company controls, then use that offshore entity to license the US patent to third parties, and the US company will not have to pay taxes on the royalties earned from the US patent as long as the royalty money stays offshore. To make matters worse, if that US company gives itself a loan of that money from the offshore company, then the US company can use the offshore money and DEDUCT from its US taxes the interest the US company pays to the offshore entity, even

though in essence all the money is the US company's money! That gives the US company a DOUBLE tax break reward by parking that money offshore.

SOLUTION:

- Eliminate the tax loophole that allows US companies to avoid taxation of revenue it earns but parks offshore
- Eliminate the tax loophole that allows companies to deduct interest on money it essentially loans to itself if that borrowed money is offshore parked money
- Give companies tax incentives to bring that money back into the US to hire people and create jobs or innovate new products.

PART 2 – GOVERNMENT REFORM

5. **Increase Transparency and Accountability in Government.** Our government needs to be accountable to the people who elect it, and the only way to achieve accountability and to prevent gaming of the system is to increase transparency and access to information. Fortunately, the internet provides a great tool to do this. It is obvious to anyone who reads about the history of the financial crisis and recent events such as the MF Global collapse

(and the missing MF Global $600 million in investor funds), that there is great need for effective regulation and prosecution of those who game the system or do illegal deeds. We need ethical enforcement of the regulations we already have as well as the creation of the new laws expressed in these Tenets for the Tea Party. This book proposes that perpetrators disgorge ill-gotten gains back into the government budget. We can promote accountability and transparency in government by:

SOLUTONS:
• Provide a web site outlining voting records and detailed accounting statements which tie congressional bills to actual expenditures and which provide "drill down" structured trees that allow citizens to obtain actual accounting details at the click of a mouse
• Provide a web site outlining each Congressman's voting history with notations indicating votes which directly benefitted large donors (or went against large donors), as well as any history of insider trading by that Congressman
• Provide a web site outlining the statistics of agency prosecutions (i.e., the SEC initiated X number of cases this year; the SEC had Y settlements this year totaling $z, etc.). This website should also give detailed information

on prosecutions and results of regulatory enforcement actions involving amounts greater than $1,000,000, and this website should notate which alleged perpetrators are donors to which Congressmen.

• Appoint people to agencies and positions who know the job, as opposed to largest campaign contributors or nepotism.

6. **Create an independent Federal watchdog reporting agency.** The huge number of government agencies, government departments, and entities receiving large direct government funds, grants and contracts makes this an area that needs constant, rigorous special oversight to be properly managed.

SOLUTION: Congress should create an independent watchdog reporting agency that methodically, and with transparency, surveys governmental departments, agencies and entities that receive direct government funds. More specifically, this independent watchdog reporting agency will be tasked to rout out and find inefficiencies, waste, corruption, and self-dealing, and this independent watchdog reporting agency will also be tasked with coming up with recommendations to Congress on effective precision methods to reduce unnecessary expenditures. This independent watchdog reporting agency will also recommend technological enhancements that will increase efficiencies. This independent watchdog reporting agency needs to be truly politics neutral and should consist of experts in several areas, including technology, accounting, finance, medicine, management, large project construction, military contracts, legal experts. etc. There should be no direct or indirect conflicts of interests or political favoritism in any watchdog reporting agency member, and a website needs to be created to highlight each reporting agency member, their contributions to the reporting agency, and the results of the reporting agency's efforts, as well as their suggestions for technology upgrades, savings and efficiencies. This independent watchdog reporting agency will become a valuable resource to Congress in making knowledgeable, non-political recommendations for efficiencies, cost savings, etc.

7. **Maintain a modern, prepared, intelligent, well equipped, lean military, that also is tasked with infrastructure security and cyber security; ensure that our veterans have proper health care and support.** Given the many articles in the news highlighting $800 bolts, it seems quite possible that we could reduce military expenditures and still

achieve United States military goals. The Department of Defense budget generally exceeds $700 billion (hard to calculate exactly since military spending these days also includes some $50 billion for Homeland Security and special appropriation bills to fund the Iraq and Afghanistan wars).

SOLUTION: The independent federal watchdog government reporting agency noted in Item 6 should be used to make independent recommendations on ways to make our military serve our needs in the most cost-effective manner.

8.   **Public employee benefits should not be greater that what the public sector offers.** No one getting a pension in excess of $100,000 should be allowed to "double-dip" by collecting a second pension. All existing government pension amounts over $100,000 should be taxed at a much higher rate, and no state should allow such high pensions to be tax free.

9. **Common Sense Priorities for our National Budget**. Our National Budget needs to have some common sense priorities. The priorities should be set to lead to a better future for the NATION, not any particular party, constituency or candidate. Hearings on baseball are a waste of national resources when there are jobless people and homes are being foreclosed on. Hearings where Congressmen give speeches instead of

pose questions to those brought before them are a waste of resources – we need open-minded, creative problem solving, not posturing. If everyone's mind is already made up based on party lines, the hearings become a wasteful mockery that we cannot afford. Making sure money flows to donors/friends while worthwhile endeavors (such as our once leading, innovative, job-creating space program or valuable news sources such as NPR) are threatened, is not in the best interests of the American people.

SOLUTION: The independent federal watchdog government reporting agency noted in Item 6 should be used to make independent recommendations on ways to make our priorities match our needs in the most cost-effective manner.

PART 3 – CREATING JOBS

10. Energy Independence generating job growth. We need to become energy independent, but without undue danger to public health or the environment. Let's avoid another gulf spill and let's not let shale fracking or nuclear power become another gulf spill (or worse). Let's not manipulate people's need for work as an excuse to abuse the environment – we should be able to accomplish both – sensibly and safely – but we need honesty first and foremost to be able to really solve our problems effectively.

SOLUTION: The independent federal watchdog government reporting agency noted in Item 6 should be used to make independent recommendations on cost-effective ways to make the United States energy independent in a manner that creates jobs without sacrificing our environment.

11. **Promote innovation generating job growth**. Our country has been blessed with brilliant innovators and entrepreneurs, such as Steve Jobs. We need to harness some of this brilliance for the benefit of our country – improving our country's infrastructure and efficiencies. Some of this is the role of the President, to lead innovators in wanting to contribute to our country's overall welfare.

SOLUTION: The independent federal watchdog government reporting agency noted in Item 6 should have brainstorming sessions with our greatest innovators, and use these sessions to be used to make independent recommendations on cost-effective ways to keep the United States on the leading edge of innovation, thereby creating jobs and also improving our country's infrastructure and efficiencies. I believe many of our country's innovators will voluntarily help us. It should be seen as a reward that a great innovator is asked to serve our government on task forces to improve life for everyone – we need to make sure people know it is an HONOR to be chosen innovative enough to serve our country. Alternatively, If we can mandate jury duty, perhaps we can mandate some form of government service from our best innovators, in the form of brainstorming sessions in special government task forces.

12. **Revise legislation to promote job growth**
There are many small businesses located near each other that can't afford one full time employee with benefits. There are also many people currently employed who need fulltime work, rather than part time work.

SOLUTION: Legislation should be adopted that permits small businesses to join together to hire one full-time employee with benefits, with the benefit costs shared between the two employers. The Unemployment Offices could be used to assist employers in finding other employer partners seeking similar skillsets in an employee, and insurance company, labor and unemployment regulations should be amended to enable this sharing of an employee's health insurance, worker's compensation, payroll, and unemployment costs.

13. **Compassion for the truly needy**. Let's not devolve into a heartless society that ignores the needy of our extended American family that simply aren't as lucky as we are. This is different than rewarding those who don't wish to work but could. Let's create programs that help people work to their abilities, and support those that simply, through serious disability or injury or age, can't.

14. **Stimulate entrepreneurship and sense of community by providing some level of health care**. Studies have shown that entrepreneurship is actually higher in some Scandinavian countries because a person doesn't need to choose between having insurance for healthcare and starting their own business. Similarly, some minimum level of health care should be provided free of charge to each US citizen on a sliding scale based on income. More specifically, every citizen falling below a certain income level would receive basic care free of charge, with additional health care insurance available to low income individuals at a subsidized cost. As a person's income level increases, the amount of free health care available without purchasing insurance decreases, and the cost

of that additional insurance coverage increases as a person's income level increases. In this manner, every US citizen has some level of health care, with the poorest people getting basic care for free, while the wealthiest billionaire class people need to pay more for their insurance and are entitled to no subsidies whatsoever. Any US citizen choosing not to purchase the additional insurance required of their income level (which provides coverage beyond the basics) is then on their own/dependent on private charity/dependent on their individual state of residency if instances occur for which they would have needed the additional insurance. Non-US citizens are not entitled to any health care subsidies unless (a) they have a bona fide H-1 VISA AND (b) their employer pays 50% of the subsidy (thereby encouraging employment of US citizens first). The system could perhaps run most efficiently if each citizen were provided with a health care account or debit card which could be credited by the medical provider for each use, up to the annual cap of basic insurance.

Whenever free healthcare is mentioned, this question quite reasonably follows – how do we pay for it? The following sections addresses this question.

PART 4 – REFORM THE HEALTH CARE INDUSTRY

15. **Reform the Healthcare Industry**: As previously stated, some minimum level of health care should be provided free of charge to each US citizen on a sliding scale based on income. More specifically, every citizen falling below a certain income level would receive basic care free of charge, with additional health care insurance available to low income individuals at a subsidized cost. As a person's income level increases, the amount of free health care available without purchasing insurance decreases, and the cost of that additional insurance coverage increases as a person's income level increases. In this manner, every US citizen has some level of health care, with the poorest people getting basic care for free, while the wealthiest billionaire class people need to pay more for their insurance and are entitled to no subsidies whatsoever. Any US citizen choosing not to purchase the additional insurance required of their income level (which provides coverage beyond the basics) is then on their own/dependent on private charity/dependent on their individual state of residency if instances occur for which they would have needed the additional insurance. Non-US citizens are not entitled to

any health care subsidies unless (a) they have a bona fide H-1 VISA AND (b) their employer pays 50% of the subsidy (thereby encouraging employment of US citizens first). The system could perhaps run most efficiently if each citizen were provided with a health care account or debit card which could be credited by the medical provider for each use, up to the annual cap of the basic insurance amount.

In addition, from an administrative and cost-savings perspective, the health care system/industry needs to be seriously reformed - there is huge waste, self- dealing and corruption in the system. All one has to do is watch CNBC's "American Greed" TV program to hear about doctors performing unneeded surgeries to get Medicare reimbursement, etc. On the other hand, many good doctors complain that the insurance companies are now more in charge of health care decisions than the doctor himself. Both these situations need to be addressed for any health care system to work.

The independent federal watchdog government reporting agency noted in Item 6 should be used to make independent recommendations on the true status of health care and what improvements can be made.

●For example, the insurance reimbursement process is needlessly hard to manage for doctors and patients alike. One does not need to be too cynical to note that anything that slows the reimbursement system down benefits the insurance company – keep in mind that insurance companies get interest on the money in their coffers until the insurance company uses that money to pay off claims. The pace and procedure of reimbursements should be far better regulated and almost immediate. For example, some types of illnesses require frequent blood work – why wouldn't an insurance card work like a credit card in that instance? Why the long delays for reimbursement in that case?

●As another example, the health care industry, in part due to privacy requirements, suffers greatly from a lack of intelligent use of technology.

●Some people advocate capping malpractice jury awards as a way of keeping costs down. However, in a case of a serious malpractice, such as where a child is seriously disabled and injured for life due to a doctor's malpractice, such an arbitrary cap on jury awards serves to place the child on state and federal welfare rather than have the perpetrator – the careless doctor – pay for the damages he created. Moreover, Texas already has a cap on malpractice insurance, and it hasn't worked well – the Texas example makes it doubtful that capping jury damages would have any material positive effects on health care costs, since the benefit of the malpractice jury award caps imposed by Texas have accrued solely to the insurance companies, not the policy holders; insurance companies continue to make record profits while insurance rates rise. Finally, Texas has fewer doctors per 1000 people than does Massachusetts, a state without such a malpractice jury award cap, so it does not appear that having a malpractice jury award cap would encourage more medical practices.

PART 5 – SUPPORT HOUSING & REDUCE FORECLOSURES

Sadly many people have lost their jobs (or were struck by severe illness without adequate health insurance) and lost their homes at a time when housing values have plummeted, and everyone was trying to sell their homes at the same time. House values have plummeted for many reasons. One is that lax mortgage writing practices were encouraged by the derivative securities known as collateralized debt obligations. These derivative securities were sometimes rated as investment grade by the rating agencies, even when the mortgage debt the derivative securities referenced were subprime. This investment grade rating provided a robust investor market, and those bundling mortgages into collateralized debt obligations needed an ongoing supply of mortgages as a foundation. Coincidentally, our government encouraged relaxing the mortgage writing standards required by Fannie Mae and Freddie Mac, enabling more mortgages to be written for borrowers, even for borrowers having questionable resources to repay the mortgages. At the same time, with mortgages being easy to obtain, house prices kept on rising due to increased demand, and some people discovered that flipping homes was a way to make an income, and in essence became speculators in the housing market. These speculators were caught surprised when the housing market crashed, but their drive to earn money did also help to create the housing bubble. This last group, the speculators, are not the group that the following proposals are written to help. It is those people who bought their home as a long-term home, not to flip, that this proposal intends to help (although if the home the speculator intended to flip is their primary residence, then this proposal would help them as well).

Right now, banks have foreclosed on more homes than they can maintain. Banks do not wish to carry homes they can't resell on their books. Foreclosing on a home is also an expensive process for the banks. The following proposals would help reduce the foreclosure rate and therefore help support the housing market until more jobs are created.

SOLUTIONS:

16. **Create One-Time Mortgage Interest Reduction for Fannie Mae/Freddie Mac Mortgages.** Many homeowners have timely made their mortgage payments but because of the costs of refinancing, the loss in value of their homes, or their job situation, they would not be able to refinance. This book proposes that every Fannie Mae/Freddie Mac backed mortgage have an addendum added to it, that would give every homeowner who has timely paid his mortgage for at least one year, the option to elect to refinance his mortgage at the current market interest rate without paying fees, without having an appraisal, without having to provide any financial information and without filling out extensive paperwork. This option will help more people stay in their homes, reduce the

overall foreclosure burden on the banks, reduce the paperwork burden, and give the banks an opportunity to thank the tax payers who bailed them out when the banks needed help, in essence a virtuous circle. This will also leave some homeowners with more money for home improvements, to purchase more goods, and otherwise stimulate the economy. This option would only be available on the primary residence of the borrower.

17. **Create Convertible Mortgage-to-Rent-to-Mortgage Option Prior to Foreclosure.** There are sadly people who simply can't make their mortgage payments but could make a significantly smaller rent payment. This book proposes that homeowners have an-easy-to-exercise option to convert their mortgage to a rental agreement with the bank, at half the mortgage rate. The rental agreement would be a standard addendum in a simple form provided by Fannie Mae/Freddie Mac for their backed mortgages. If the homeowner exercises his option to convert his mortgage into a lease, then for the next three years, the homeowner would have an option to convert the lease back to a mortgage under the original mortgage terms. If both parties agree, the home can be sold in that 3 year period, with any amount in excess of any

remaining mortgage going to the homeowner. If the owner does not exercise his option or falls materially behind on his rent, then the traditional foreclosure process could then be instituted. In this manner, the homeowner can stay in their home and hopefully be able to reconvert back to a mortgage within the three year period, giving the homeowner a bit of a breather to get back on their feet, and the bank is not burdened with another foreclosure to maintain.

PART 6 – NONPROFITS NEED TO DO THEIR PART TOO

18. **Eliminate Gaming of the Nonprofit Deduction/Tax-Free Status.** The fastest growing sector in the US economy is the nonprofit sector. The nonprofit sector accounts for approximately 10% of the United States economy (measured by gross domestic product (GDP)). It is important to note that being a nonprofit does not mean that high wages can't be paid to executive directors or lead staff that run the nonprofit – in fact, salaries at some nonprofit organizations can be quite generous for executive directors and lead fundraisers. Some of the larger nonprofit CEOs and Executive Directors in fact can get paid salaries in excess of $2 million per year. In 2008, the charitable nonprofit

sector employed over 13.5 million people (around 10% of the US workforce) earning almost $540 billion in annual wages – an average of $40,000 per employee. Also, the umbrella of what can be called a nonprofit and hence qualify for tax free donations, etc. is quite broad. Given the tax benefits and opportunities to game the nonprofit tax-free system, it is not surprising that the nonprofit sector is growing so quickly.

Nonprofits do many good and important things for our communities and environment. However, there is no accountability or requirement that a nonprofit be efficient in what it does in order to maintain its nonprofit status. While no doubt some nonprofits are quite efficient, other nonprofits have significant parts of their donations going to administrative overhead rather than serving the needy, etc. Therefore, a key question in analyzing the nonprofit sector is: Does the tax benefit nonprofits enjoy for themselves and their donors outweigh the actual cost of the services these nonprofits provide?

As additional background, the largest annual fundraising entity in the US is not the Red Cross, not the United Way, not the Sierra Club - it is religious organizations, raising millions – even billions - of tax free dollars per year. Religious organizations receiving tax free dollars are not required to report the exact amount of tax free donations they receive. What is clear is that no taxes are paid by the donor or any religious entity on any of those millions/billions of dollars of tax free donations. In addition, there is no accountability at all for how tax free money raised by any religious organization is used. There is no requirement that the religious organization use any of that money here in the US, rather than overseas. There is no calculation of how many people actually attend a particular church/temple/mosque verses the annual tax free benefit. There is no requirement that any religious organization meet any minimum legal behavioral standards (for example, no requirement exists that a religious organization report child molestation or risk losing its tax free status).

This tax free status for religious organizations is as true on the state level as on the federal level. Religious organizations are among the largest real estate holders in the US, owning possibly over a trillion dollars of tax free real estate, and no property taxes are paid on any of that real estate held by religious organizations. Tax-free property means that all religious organizations enjoy the use of roads, firemen, policeman, without paying any state or local taxes to support them. In part because there is not yet a cap on how much real estate is tax free for religious nonprofits, there are religious organizations owning prime ocean view mansions and multiple prime properties in expensive neighborhoods, and these properties are not always open to all members of their own congregation or to the public.

Background as to how this Nonprofit Tax Exemption Came About: The justification for tax free status for nonprofits has two underpinnings: (a) for religious nonprofits only - the separation of church and state issue – to guard against the state taxing a religion out of existence; and (b) for all nonprofits, we want to encourage nonprofits generally (religious and non-religious) to do social services in the US, so the US government doesn't have to provide those social services directly.

SOLUTIONS:

First: This book proposes that the independent federal government reporting agency noted in Item 6 should be used to make an independent assessment and quantification of the actual amount of taxes that would have been received by the IRS had the nonprofit deductions not been available, and that the federal government reporting agency should also list which nonprofits receive more than $50 million in tax free donations each year, along with the salaries of the top 5 most highly paid employees and with an estimate of the tax free donations that nonprofit received in aggregate for the year. No citizen can properly voice his opinion on this issue unless he knows the magnitude of the taxes NOT being paid. It is quite possible that if all nonprofits paid some taxes, the tax rate for ALL of us could be lower.

Depending on the results of that study, here are two alternative solutions:

Alternative 1: This is the most drastic alternative – we could entirely eliminate the nonprofit tax deduction in reference to ALL charities, whether religious or non-religious, whether for the arts, education, or the needy. Once we have a balanced budget we can reconsider re- instituting these deductions, but the reality is, if someone really wants to support an organization they will; if they are solely supporting the organization for the tax deduction then it would appear that they don't believe all that strongly in the mission of the nonprofit they purport to support.

ALTERNATIVE 2: This is a less drastic solution than Alternative 1, but would still eliminate millions, if not billions, of tax loopholes.

● Cap all tax free real estate to $100 million for ANY nonprofit (i.e., a nonprofit can own more than $100 million in real estate, but the nonprofit would have to pay property taxes on the excess real estate owned over $100 million). The study by the independent federal reporting agency should look in to how much tax-free real estate is an appropriate amount for a religious organization to operate, and their report might well indicate that a different cap would be more appropriate than the proposed $100 million cap on tax free real estate. In any event, even if the cap on tax free real estate ends up being more (or less) than $100 million, there should be a cap on tax free real estate. At a time when Congress is talking about eliminating the mortgage deduction for homeowners, it seems equitable that religious organizations owning hundreds of millions (if not trillions) of dollars of real estate should be made to pay their fair share of taxes as well. Again, a nonprofit can own more than

$100 million in real estate, but the nonprofit would have to pay property taxes on the excess real estate owned over $100 million.

• Only donations actually used here in the US should be tax free; if donated money is to be used outside of the United States, then the donation is no longer tax-free.   Recall that one principle justifying nonprofit status is that we taxpayers give tax-free status to nonprofits so the US government doesn't need to provide some social services directly as a government. This second justification, the provision of social services here in the US so the US government doesn't need to provide those social services, simply can't hold true if the tax free money leaves the US and isn't used here in the United States.   Tax-free money sent overseas by the nonprofit does NOT provide social services to the needy here in the US. At a minimum, any tax free dollars (whether from property tax savings or non-taxable donations) that are sent overseas by the nonprofit should be taxed when those dollars leave the US, because the American people aren't getting the social services benefit here in the US of those dollars. This book proposes that this requirement, that the tax-free status is preserved only for money used here in the US, applies to all nonprofits, whether religious or non-religious. Once we have a balanced budget we can reconsider re- instituting these deductions for international purposes, but the reality is, if someone really wants to support an international effort they will; if they are solely supporting the international effort for the tax deduction then it would appear that they don't believe all that strongly in the mission of the international effort they purport to support.

• There should be more transparency on how tax free money is used. All nonprofits should have the same disclosure obligations to the IRS. Right now, nonreligious organizations have to disclose much more to the IRS than religious organizations. The quid pro quo for tax free status should be annual reporting requirements to maintain tax free status. All taxpayers should have easy internet access to see how much of those tax-free billions are NOT being reinvested in their communities and home country. If the majority of the tax-free donations are being used to support administrative overhead (multimillion CEO salaries for example) instead of feeding the poor (for example), this book proposes that the tax payers should have easy access to that information.

• All religious organizations should be encouraged to at least voluntarily lead by example and pay their fair share of property taxes to show support for the police, fireman, and teachers, of all faiths, that have similarly also diligently provided community service for so many years.

PART 7 – RESOLVE THE ILLEGAL IMMIGRATION ISSUE – REALISTICALLY

19. **Resolve the Illegal Immigration Issue Realistically.** This is not an easy problem, but it is important to note that states such as Georgia, with strict anti-illegal immigrant laws, have farmers complaining that now they are forced to leave fruit rotting on the fields because these farmers can no longer find workers to pick them. Realistically, our agriculture industry needs migrant workers, who have shown themselves to be a hard working, effective solution for our agriculture field work.

SOLUTION: This book proposes a treaty with Mexico, enabling US agricultural employers to employ those migrant workers who wish to work in the United States, at a negotiated wage, solely for our agricultural industry, under a new US-MEX Labor treaty. For migrant workers falling under that treaty, this book proposes that the migrant workers would be issued a special Visa limiting them to agriculture work, and this book also proposes that the Mexican government needs to pick up 25-50% of the health care tab for those migrant workers (which 25-50% can be payable in Mexico-sourced oil at then current market rates, thereby assisting the US in its energy independence goals as well).

PART 8 – WE ALL MUST DO OUR PART

20. **We Must All do Our Part**. We need ethical enforcement of the regulations we already have, and we need EVERYONE, each of us, whether an individual, the government, and even the nonprofits, each and every one, to stop gaming the system. It is our honor to live in the United States with our freedom and equality, and it is our duty as citizens to live and contribute in an ethical manner, and to peacefully, diligently and with great care express our needs, concerns and ideas to our government leaders.

It is the intention of this book that the proposals, ideas and information in this book are of help to you in your thinking process. These 20 solutions are suggested thinking points, starting places, and hopefully the community discussion that ensues around each solution will generate new ideas and constructive answers to the very real problems we Americans now face.